Original title:

Nurturing Creativity

Editor: Theodor Taimla

Author: Isabella Ilves

ISBN HARDBACK: 978-9916-763-76-6

ISBN PAPERBACK: 978-9916-763-77-3

handwritten notes of the cosmos

Stars scribble secrets in the night,
Galaxies dance with soft delight.
Comets trace paths in the dark,
Each a whisper, each a spark.

Planets spin in graceful arcs,
Time drifts gently, never stark.
Moonlight kisses the quiet sea,
Echoes of life, wild and free.

Nebulae bloom, colors collide,
Infinite wonders, far and wide.
In this vast expanse, we see,
Handwritten notes of destiny.

Dreams unfurl like solar sails,
Guided by unseen trails.
Through the void, we chase the light,
Searching for truth in the night.

Every heartbeat, every breath,
Links us deeper, life or death.
In the cosmos, we find our role,
Handwritten scripts of the soul.

Echoes of Vision

In the silence, whispers call,
Fleeting shadows rise and fall.
Chasing dreams like morning light,
A canvas painted, bold and bright.

Through the fog, a glimpse of truth,
Stories woven, seeds of youth.
Every heartbeat, every sigh,
Echoes linger, never die.

The Echo of Elysium

In fields of gold, the whispers play,
Soft as dawn, they greet the day.
Each blade of grass, a gentle sigh,
The echo of dreams drifting by.

Petals fall like memories sweet,
Dance of moments, soft and fleet.
Beneath the boughs, shadows intertwine,
Elysium's glow, so divine.

Laughter mingles with the breeze,
A symphony sung by the trees.
Hope's bright hue paints the sky,
In this realm, we learn to fly.

Time stands still, the heartbeats blend,
In the silence, we comprehend.
Every echo finds a home,
In the whispers, we freely roam.

Elysium's light, a guiding flame,
Chasing shadows, we call its name.
In the depths, our spirits find,
A sanctuary, intertwined.

A Symphony of Whimsy

Notes of laughter fill the air,
Dancing petals everywhere.
A melody of pure delight,
Twinkling stars that shine at night.

Twirling leaves in vibrant hues,
Nature's stage, a grand muse.
Playful winds, they twist and twirl,
In this symphony, dreams unfurl.

Radiance of Revelations

Underneath a brilliant sky,
Wisdom flows as time drifts by.
Truths unveiled, like morning dew,
Reflecting all that we pursue.

Awakening hearts in the dawn,
Lessons learned, and fears withdrawn.
Shining paths lead us to see,
The radiance of mystery.

Dreamers dance on ancient ground,
In the silence, answers found.
Each revelation, a spark ignites,
Illuminating hidden sights.

Stars align with gentle grace,
In their light, we find our place.
Fleeting shadows fade away,
Radiance blesses every day.

In the sacredness of night,
We embrace the soft, pure light.
Through the veil, we seek to know,
The revelations, we bestow.

Tapestry of Dreams

Threads of hope in colors bold,
Stories waiting to be told.
Weaving visions, heart to heart,
In each stitch, a brand new start.

Embroidered paths of joy and pain,
Sunshine's warmth and pouring rain.
Every dream a vibrant line,
In this tapestry, we shine.

Gardens of Inspiration

In the quiet gleam of dawn,
Petals whisper tales untold,
Colors dance in morning's breath,
Dreams awaken, bright and bold.

Beneath the shade of ancient trees,
Thoughts like flowers bloom and grow,
Nature's canvas fills the soul,
With every seed that we sow.

Rivers hum a gentle tune,
Over stones both smooth and worn,
Inspiration flows like water,
In gardens where the hope is born.

Sunlight weaves a golden thread,
Through branches reaching for the sky,
Nurtured by the hands of time,
In this space, our spirits fly.

Here in this eternal place,
Ideas flourish, wild and free,
A tapestry of dreams unveiled,
In gardens of eternity.

Colors Beyond the Ordinary

Palette bright, the world displayed,
Magic in the hues conveyed.
Emerald greens and sapphire skies,
A vibrant feast for eager eyes.

Crimson sunsets, golden dawns,
Nature's beauty, endlessly drawn.
Beyond the gray, a vivid spree,
Colors dance, wild and free.

Whispers of the Imagination

In the garden of dreams we grow,
Seeds of thought begin to flow.
Colors dance and stories weave,
Whispers of what we believe.

With every stroke, creation sings,
Boundless realms, the heart takes wing.
Visions bloom, bright and bold,
Imagination, our treasures unfold.

Chasing shadows, light embraced,
Fleeting moments cannot be chased.
In the silence, ideas ignite,
Guiding us into the night.

Painting worlds with vibrant hues,
Dreaming paths, we can't refuse.
Each whisper calls to the brave,
The imagination, a sacred wave.

With every heartbeat, stories rise,
Infinite tales beneath the skies.
In the echoes, we find our way,
Whispers of truth, here to stay.

Echoes of Untamed Dreams

Whispers call from distant shores,
Where starlit nights find restless hearts,
Chasing shadows of the past,
As the moonlight softly departs.

Visions dance in midnight's glow,
Beneath the vast and endless sky,
Each echo tells a secret tale,
Of dreams that dare to soar and fly.

In the silence of the night,
Creativity knows no bounds,
Unraveled hopes like fragile threads,
In each heartbeat, freedom sounds.

Awakened by the pulse of stars,
We wander through the cosmic seam,
With every step, the journey spreads,
Echoes of our untamed dream.

Together we will break the dawn,
Letting go of chains that bind,
In the realm of possibilities,
Our courage, vivid and aligned.

The Tapestry of Thought

Woven strands of bright ideas,
Interlaced in colors bold,
A tapestry of endless dreams,
Each thread a story to be told.

Moments captured, swift as light,
In a dance of minds entwined,
Imagination takes its flight,
In the richness of the blind.

Patterns form and break apart,
Textures weave through time and space,
In the fabric of our thoughts,
We find our truth, we find our grace.

A needle plunges deep within,
Stitching memories with intent,
Creating visions that inspire,
Every piece a gift well sent.

As we journey through our days,
Let creativity unfold,
In the tapestry of thought,
Life's masterpiece will be our gold.

Seeds of Originality

In fertile minds, the seeds are sown,
A spark that sets the world ablaze,
Originality takes root,
In uncharted, daring ways.

Curiosity, the silent guide,
Leading paths to realms anew,
With every question, answers bloom,
In the garden of the true.

Cultivated with care and love,
Each idea a vibrant sprout,
Challenging the status quo,
Opening paths that we think about.

The wind carries whispers loud,
Of visions yet to manifest,
In the soil of our passions,
We nurture dreams, we invest.

As seasons change and chaos reigns,
We stand firm through stormy weather,
For in our hearts, the seeds we've sown,
Will break through earth, grow tall together.

Breath of Innovation

In shadows where ideas bloom,
A spark ignites the silent room.
Whispers dance on the cool night air,
Dreams awaken, bold and rare.

With every step, the path unfurls,
A canvas bright, the future swirls.
Thoughts collide, a vibrant phase,
Invention's light sets hearts ablaze.

Through trials faced, through doubts and fears,
We carve our way amidst the cheers.
Each failure molds what we create,
A testament to change and fate.

Eyes fixed ahead, we break the mold,
In vision bright, our truth unfold.
Together we shall rise and seize,
The breath of change, the sweet, sweet breeze.

With hands united, we will strive,
To keep the spark of hope alive.
In every heart, innovation's call,
A symphony that binds us all.

Sculpting in the Void

In silent space where whispers die,
We carve our dreams, just you and I.
With each chisel, visions rise,
Forming worlds beneath the skies.

Fingers trace the endless night,
Churning shadows into light.
With every stroke, a life begins,
In the void, we find our sins.

Fragments dance in ethereal glow,
Shaping stories only we know.
Echoes linger, soft and sweet,
In empty spaces, art shall meet.

Each creation, a breath of time,
Born from chaos, making rhyme.
In the silence, we build anew,
A sculpture shaped by me and you.

Together here, where thoughts collide,
We forge our truth and turn the tide.
In every corner, beauty calls,
Sculpting life as darkness falls.

Fluttering Brushstrokes

On canvas wide, the colors soar,
With brush in hand, we explore.
Each stroke a whisper, soft and true,
Painting dreams in shades of blue.

Fluttering hearts, in rhythm dance,
As colors mingle, they take a chance.
A splash of joy, a hint of pain,
In every layer, love's refrain.

Gentle hands weave tales of light,
A tapestry of day and night.
With every flutter, life takes hold,
Stories waiting to be told.

The palette sings in vibrant hues,
As inspiration finds its muse.
We touch the canvas, hearts aglow,
Through fluttering strokes, emotions flow.

In every piece, a world resides,
Boundless journeys, in dreams we glide.
Together, we'll create our fate,
With fluttering brushstrokes, we elevate.

Harmonies of the Unseen

In whispers soft, the music swells,
A tune that only silence tells.
Notes entwine in shadows deep,
Where secrets lost in silence sleep.

Through hidden realms, the rhythms play,
An unseen dance in shades of gray.
With every breath, a chord is struck,
In melodies, we find our luck.

Between the lines, the echoes sing,
Of barren lands and budding spring.
A harmony that fills the air,
Uniting souls in subtle flair.

In every heart, a song resides,
A truth that time and space abides.
With silent harmonies, we sway,
In thoughts profound, we find our way.

Together, let our voices blend,
In unseen chords, around the bend.
For in this symphony of dreams,
We craft the world, or so it seems.

Whispers of Imagination

In the quiet night, whispers glide,
Thoughts take flight, a gentle tide.
Colors dance in the mind's embrace,
Creating worlds in empty space.

Stars above begin to gleam,
Carrying the weight of a dream.
Voices soft, like a lover's sigh,
In this realm, we learn to fly.

Every shadow hides a tale,
In the dark, we set our sail.
Mysteries wrapped in a soft embrace,
Among the clouds, we find our place.

Echoes linger, spirits roam,
In these thoughts, we find our home.
Imagination's boundless sea,
A treasure trove, wild and free.

Embers of Innovation

From ashes rise the embers bright,
Sparks igniting the canvas of night.
Ideas flicker, bold and clear,
A vision born from hope and fear.

With every breath, a chance to create,
Breaking the chains, we elevate.
Innovation flows like a mighty stream,
Nurturing the heart of every dream.

Together we forge, hand in hand,
Building bridges across the land.
In the face of doubt, we stand tall,
With courage to answer the call.

Embers glow and warmth they bring,
As we rise, we learn to sing.
The future glimmers, bright and grand,
A tapestry woven by our hand.

The Canvas of Dreams

Brush in hand, colors unfold,
On a canvas, stories told.
Every stroke a tale to share,
Imagination dances in the air.

Colors swirl in vibrant grace,
Each hue a glimpse of a hidden place.
Dreams awaken, vivid and bright,
Painting shadows with beams of light.

Every vision a work of art,
A reflection of the beating heart.
Boundless realms in every hue,
Inviting the wanderer to breakthrough.

On this canvas, hope takes flight,
In the darkest times, find the light.
With every dream, we leave a mark,
Creating magic from the dark.

Seeds of Inspiration

In the soil of the mind, seeds are sown,
In the quiet heart, ideas grown.
With gentle hands, we nurture fate,
Holding tight to dreams we create.

Every whisper, a promise made,
In the sunlight, fears will fade.
From small beginnings, greatness blooms,
Filling the world with sweet perfumes.

Harvest moments, gather near,
Inspiration flows, bright and clear.
Planting thoughts like wildflowers,
Breathing life into the hours.

In the garden of the soul, we find,
Visions woven through mankind.
With love and courage, we take a stand,
And watch our dreams spread across the land.

Sketches of Untapped Potential

In the shadows of our dreams,
Where hope begins to grow,
Sketches wait to come alive,
Waiting for the chance to show.

Beyond the walls of doubt,
Vibrant colors start to blend,
Imagination takes its flight,
A journey without end.

With each stroke of courage,
We carve what lies within,
Crafting paths to futures bright,
Where possibilities begin.

In whispers of the heart,
Lie visions yet to find,
Every dream a canvas wide,
For the daring soul and kind.

Let us dance with the unknown,
Embrace what's on the brink,
For in the depths of silence,
We learn what thoughts can think.

Serenity in the Storm of Imagination

In the chaos of the mind,
A gentle breeze does flow,
Whispers lift the spirit high,
While restless thoughts wind slow.

Clouds of doubt may gather round,
Yet stars begin to shine,
In the storm of all we think,
There's solace too divine.

Creativity ignites bright,
In thunder's wild embrace,
The tempest fuels our passions,
While calmness holds its place.

Each wave of thought and feeling,
A dance of storm and peace,
Amidst the swirling chaos,
We find our true release.

So let the currents carry us,
Through peaks of joy and grief,
For within this stormy heart,
Lies a tender, quiet belief.

The Palette of Human Experience

Colors collide in the heart's embrace,
Joy and sorrow wear a vivid face.
Moments painted with laughter and tears,
Each stroke tells a tale through the years.

Shades of love dance in the light,
Soft whispers turn wrongs to right.
In every hue, a story unfolds,
The richness of life, a canvas bold.

From the darkness, bright sparks are drawn,
After the night comes the hopeful dawn.
A spectrum of dreams in vibrant bloom,
A gallery of memories fills the room.

Each day a brush with the unknown,
Emotions blend like seeds we've sown.
Through the chaos, beauty can be seen,
A masterpiece forged in the spaces between.

With every heartbeat, a fresh design,
A tapestry woven with threads divine.
The palette of life is vast and wide,
In every color, the truth can hide.

Transformations of the Mind

Thoughts like rivers flow and twist,
Currents of dreams that can't be missed.
Epiphanies spring from restless nights,
In the stillness, wisdom ignites.

Mirrors reflect the soul's desire,
Changing shapes that never tire.
Shadows linger, but light breaks through,
Old beliefs fade, and the new shines true.

Ideas turn like autumn leaves,
Whispers of change that the heart weaves.
In the silence, revelations bloom,
Transformations quiet the mind's gloom.

Past and present collide in grace,
Awakening visions we can't erase.
An evolution of thoughts, profound,
In sparking minds, new worlds are found.

Adapting to every fleeting chance,
With every shift, the spirit's dance.
In the canvas of thought, bright and vast,
We find our path, as shadows pass.

Beyond the Borders of Thought

A realm where dreams take to the skies,
Limitless journeys in reason's disguise.
Ideas break free from society's mold,
Voices of the heart, fearless and bold.

Questions linger on the edge of night,
Seeking truths that guide our flight.
Beyond the borders, where silence speaks,
A symphony of thoughts, if only we seek.

Fleeting moments of clarity shine,
In the chaos, a design divine.
The mind stretches like an endless sea,
A voyage into the depths of 'me.'

Looking past walls that confine and cage,
Exploring the wisdom of every age.
In the labyrinth of consciousness vast,
We unravel the threads of future and past.

In this expanse, we're never alone,
Every pulse and whisper, a known tone.
Beyond the borders, our spirits glide,
Finding solace in the thoughts that abide.

The Sanctuary of Original Ideas

Within the heart lies a sacred space,
A sanctuary where thoughts embrace.
Whispers of truth in gentle flight,
Crafting wonders under moonlight.

Silent musings begin to emerge,
As inspiration flows like a surge.
In solitude, ideas find their voice,
Shaping dreams that ignite choice.

Layers of passion gently unfold,
Unique visions that refuse to be told.
The spark of creation dances awake,
Nurturing seeds that we dare to make.

In this haven, innovation thrives,
Fading noise, where the spirit strives.
Ideas blossom like flowers in spring,
In the garden of thought, life's offerings.

Here, each thought is a brushstroke found,
Painting possibilities that astound.
In this sanctuary, we dare to roam,
Finding the magic that calls us home.

The Mosaic of Thought

In a garden where ideas bloom,
Colors dance, dispelling gloom.
Words like petals, soft and bright,
Crafting patterns in the light.

Questions weave through dawn's embrace,
Seeking wisdom, finding place.
Each fragment, a story told,
A tapestry, both brave and bold.

Reflections in the still water,
Dreams emerge; they twist and falter.
Guided by the stars above,
Minds connect in threads of love.

Voices rise, a symphony,
Echoing in harmony.
Thoughts entwined, they swirl and glide,
In the heart, where truths abide.

Light and shadow, dance in time,
Fragments penned in simple rhyme.
A mosaic, ever growing,
In the silence, ideas flowing.

Chasing Starlit Fantasies

Underneath the endless sky,
Dreams like constellations lie.
Whispers of the night unfold,
Stories waiting to be told.

With each breath, the cosmos gleams,
Painted worlds and silent screams.
Wishes carried on the breeze,
Twinkling hopes among the trees.

Eager hearts pursue the light,
In the dark, they chase the sight.
Every sparkle, a guiding flame,
Leading wanderers to claim.

Adventurers on paths unknown,
Through the stardust, seeds are sown.
Every step, a dance with fate,
As they weave, they serenade.

In the quiet, magic hums,
Chasing after all it becomes.
Starlit dreams in every glance,
Weaving hopes in endless dance.

Heartbeats of Invention

In the workshop, shadows play,
Hands create, in night and day.
Ideas spark, ignite the air,
Bringing visions into care.

Every tool, a trusted friend,
Crafting wonders without end.
Heartbeats echo, rhythmic sound,
Moments lost and then found.

Dreamers gathered, minds collide,
Inventions born, with hope beside.
Unraveled thoughts like strands of silk,
Crafting futures, rich as milk.

Each mistake, a step to climb,
In the chaos, finding rhyme.
Innovation's gentle call,
Reaching out to one and all.

In whispers soft, ideas grow,
Through perseverance, we will know.
Heartbeats pulse, a steady plan,
Inventing worlds, we'll take a stand.

The Whispering Tide

Waves that crash upon the shore,
Secrets linger, tales of yore.
With each ebb, a story fades,
In the depths, the ocean wades.

Moonlight dances on the sea,
Telling tales of mystery.
Whispers carry on the breeze,
Gentle songs among the trees.

Seagulls cry, a distant call,
As the tide begins to fall.
Salty air, a warm embrace,
Nature's rhythm, timeless grace.

Footprints left on sandy shores,
Each step opens hidden doors.
In the silence, hearts collide,
Listening to the whispering tide.

Harmony in every wave,
Lessons from the sea, we crave.
As the horizon meets the sky,
In the moment, we will fly.

The Chronicle of Artistic Flights

In colors bold, the canvas sings,
Brush strokes dance like whispered dreams.
A palette rich with life it brings,
A story told in silent themes.

The artist's heart, a world so wide,
With every mark, emotions fly.
In shadows deep, in light's bright tide,
Creation breathes; it cannot die.

Shapes entwined, the forms take flight,
Imagined realms in vibrant hues.
A journey soars into the night,
Where art ignites the soul's reviews.

From textured clay to sculpted stone,
Each piece alive with history.
Artistic souls no longer lone,
United through their mysteries.

As moonlight spills on gallery walls,
The echoes of each painter's sigh.
In every frame, a heart enthralls,
The chronicle of dreams gone by.

The Pulse of Unique Perspectives

In every eye, a world is found,
Unique the tales that shapes convey.
A heartbeat shared, yet profoundly sound,
Each point of view, a vibrant array.

Through lenses clear, we seek the truth,
In laughter's light and sorrow's rain.
Diverse reflections, a living proof,
Of life's rich tapestry, vast and plain.

With open minds, we venture far,
To grasp one heart, another's fate.
Each story shines, a guiding star,
Reminding us we co-create.

Perspectives shift like winds that blow,
In every whisper, sparks ignite.
Connected threads in ebb and flow,
Together weaving day and night.

Embrace the pulse, the rhythm strong,
In harmony, we rise and sway.
Through empathy, we all belong,
As unique dreams light up the way.

Threads of Storytelling

In whispers soft, the tales unfold,
Each thread a journey, rich and bold.
With every knot, a secret shared,
A tapestry of hearts laid bare.

From ancient lore to modern plot,
In every voice, the ages caught.
A woven path of hopes and fears,
Inked in laughter, smeared with tears.

The fabric stretches, colors blend,
Each chapter echoes, hearts ascend.
With every stitch, the bonds renew,
As stories shape what we pursue.

Beneath the stars, where dreams ignite,
The narrative swells, taking flight.
A dance of words, a rhythm true,
In story's weave, we find the view.

Through timeless lore, we come alive,
In every tale, a spark to strive.
Interwoven lives, like threads entwined,
In storytelling, the heart aligned.

Fragments of Infinity

In every moment, pieces shine,
Scattered bits of time and space.
A universe in patterns divine,
In stillness found, the fleeting grace.

With each whisper, echoes bloom,
Fragments scatter like dust in air.
Infinity glimpses in shallow gloom,
Where silence holds a spark to share.

Through broken shards, light filters through,
A kaleidoscope of dreams reborn.
In every heartbeat, worlds ensue,
Beyond horizons, hope is sworn.

Crystals glimmer in dusk's embrace,
As life transcends its mortal chain.
In every laugh, a truth we trace,
Fragments of infinity remain.

The cosmos whispers, tales entwined,
In every breath, the vast unseen.
Through fractured paths, we seek to find,
The threads of life that weave the dream.

Raindrops of Inspiration

Softly they fall, as whispers of dreams,
Cleansing the mind, igniting the streams.
Each drop a thought, pure and profound,
Nourishing soil where ideas are found.

In puddles they gather, reflecting the light,
Sparking the heart, lifting the sight.
They dance on rooftops, a rhythmic beat,
A melody formed where silence meets.

With every splash, creativity blooms,
Emerging from shadows, dispelling the glooms.
Raindrops of hope, like stars in the night,
Illuminating paths, guiding to light.

So let them fall, this deluge divine,
For in each droplet, new worlds intertwine.
A symphony crafted, a painter's embrace,
In the storm's gentle fury, we find our place.

The Odyssey of Thought

Journey begins in the vast open sea,
Waves of confusion, a quest to be free.
Sailing through tempests, storms raging high,
The map is uncertain, yet dreams never die.

Islands of knowledge, treasures concealed,
Charting our course, with truth as our shield.
Navigating currents, both fierce and serene,
The compass is passion, the horizon a dream.

With each passing moment, the mind expands wide,
In the whirlpool of questions, we willingly glide.
Resilience a beacon, shining so bright,
Guiding our vessel through the depth of the night.

As we forge ahead, through shadow and glare,
Curiosity whispers, urging us to dare.
An odyssey lasting, the heart and the brain,
In the tapestry woven, both joy and pain.

Flames of Passionate Creation

From embers ignited, a fire takes flight,
Colors of chaos, painting the night.
With sparks of desire, ideas ignite,
Creating a canvas, alive with delight.

Fanned by the breath of a fervent embrace,
The flames dance wildly, each movement a grace.
Crafting from ashes, something anew,
In the heat of creation, we find what is true.

Heat of the moment, where visions align,
Blazing with fervor, our passions entwine.
In the heart's furnace, dreams melt and combine,
Forging a legacy, transcending time.

With every flicker, possibilities rise,
Ascending to heights, where the spirit flies.
These flames of creation, relentless and bright,
Illuminate paths toward infinite light.

The Garden of New Beginnings

In the dawn's soft glow, fresh blooms emerge,
Whispers of hope in the warm morning surge.
Seeds of the future, buried so deep,
Awake from the slumber, their secrets to keep.

Petals unfurl, in vibrant array,
Colors and fragrances beckon the day.
Roots intertwining, growing as one,
In this garden of life, new journeys begun.

Each bud tells a tale, of trials and grace,
The beauty of struggle, a delicate trace.
In moments of stillness, reflections do bloom,
Painting a picture of light in the gloom.

With every new season, the garden will thrive,
Nurturing dreams, keeping hope alive.
So tend to your heart, let the sunshine in,
In the garden of beginnings, the journey begins.

Raindrops of Insight

Gentle whispers from the sky,
Each drop a thought that flutters by.
In puddles deep, reflections glow,
As minds awake, ideas flow.

A dance of droplets on the ground,
Where silence speaks, and dreams abound.
With every splash, a spark ignites,
In rain's embrace, the mind invites.

Beneath the gray, a canvas waits,
For strokes of light that insight creates.
The world shifts under whispered rain,
In every drop, wisdom's refrain.

From storms arise the brightest thoughts,
As nature weaves the truths we've sought.
With every patter, life's anew,
In raindrops clear, we find the view.

Flourish of the Mind

In the garden where ideas grow,
Seeds of insight begin to show.
With sunlight soft and waters pure,
Each thought takes root, ready to stir.

A tapestry of colors bright,
Blooms of wisdom in morning light.
Petals unfold with gentle grace,
Inviting dreams to take their place.

As breezes dance through leafy trees,
The whispers carry on the breeze.
In every corner, life expands,
Flourishing in creative hands.

From quiet soil to skies above,
The mind's creation, born of love.
Each bloom, a story yet untold,
In flourishing thoughts, we break the mold.

The Constellation of Ideas

In the vastness of the night,
Stars appear, shining bright.
Each one a thought, a spark divine,
A constellation, a grand design.

Connecting dots from one to another,
Ideas weave like sister and brother.
In celestial dance, they twirl and spin,
Inviting dreams to rise within.

With every glance at the midnight sky,
More stories whisper, bidding us to try.
In this tapestry of light, we see,
The boundless potential in you and me.

In every star, a path unfolds,
Guiding seekers, both young and old.
The constellations, timeless and true,
Bring forth the dreams we dare pursue.

Navigating the Dreamscape

In the realm where shadows play,
Thoughts take flight and drift away.
Through valleys deep and mountains high,
We navigate the dreams that lie.

With compass made of hopes and fears,
We journey forth through laughter and tears.
Each twist and turn, a story told,
In dreamscapes vast, brave hearts be bold.

The stars align with every breath,
Guiding souls beyond life's depth.
In whispered winds, we find our way,
Through the night and into day.

As dawn approaches, dreams may fade,
But in our hearts, the memories trade.
Navigating through what we find,
In every dream, a piece of mind.

Uncharted Waters of Imagination

Beneath the stars, a canvas spreads,
Whispers of dreams, where silence treads.
Currents of thought, drifting afar,
Navigating realms where wonders spar.

Sails of belief in a tempest's embrace,
Each wave a story, a vast, unknown space.
Colors collide, in the mind's gentle tide,
Charting a course where fantasies hide.

Voices of shadows, guided by light,
Echoing secrets that dance in the night.
Ripples of hope in the depths of the soul,
Catching the winds that make the heart whole.

Journeys unfold on horizons untamed,
Maps drawn in stardust, adventures unnamed.
With anchors of courage and sails of delight,
We voyage through dreams, 'neath the moon's silver light.

In uncharted waters, we find our true song,
Merging together, where spirits belong.
Exploring the realms of boundless design,
Our imaginations, forever entwined.

The Labyrinth of Expression

In corridors carved from the thoughts of old,
Whispers of stories in silence retold.
Twists and turns of the heart and the mind,
In the weave of our words, true meaning we find.

The echoes of laughter, the shadows of tears,
A tapestry woven from hopes and fears.
Each path that we tread, both narrow and wide,
Guides us through valleys where feelings reside.

Mirrors reflecting the depths of our soul,
In this dance of creation, we find ourselves whole.
The ink spills like rivers, the pages set free,
Revealing the labyrinth that thrives within me.

Every corner turned sparks a vision anew,
In the maze of expression, the colors break through.
We embrace the chaos, the beauty, the pain,
In this journey of words, all is gained, nothing vain.

As we navigate through this intricate place,
The heart of our stories leaves its trace.
In the labyrinth of minds, we carve out a space,
To echo our truths in a timeless embrace.

The Essence of Wonder

In the glimmer of dawn, where dreams take flight,
Children of stars dance in morning's light.
Questions like raindrops, soft on the ground,
Each one a treasure where answers are found.

The rustle of leaves sings tales of the wise,
Colors of laughter paint over the skies.
In the pulse of a moment, we stop and we see,
The essence of wonder, so wild and so free.

Every heartbeat a rhythm, each breath a new song,
In a world of enchantment, we all belong.
Finding the magic in simple delight,
As the universe beckons us, day into night.

With eyes wide open, we seek and explore,
In the whispers of nature, there's always much more.
The stories of ages, held close in our hands,
Reveal the connections that time never strands.

So cherish the moments, embrace the unseen,
For the essence of wonder lies where we've been.
In the heart of existence, we journey along,
Finding beauty in silence, and strength in our song.

Fables of the Heart

Once upon a time, in a world so bright,
Stories of love danced in the soft moonlight.
Whispers of comfort, a gentle embrace,
Fables of the heart, where dreams find their place.

In the realm of the brave, where courage is born,
Each choice we make is a new tale adorned.
With echoes of laughter and shadows of pain,
We weave our own stories, like sun and like rain.

Characters painted with each brush of grace,
In the pages of life, we discover our space.
From the depths of despair to the heights of delight,
Every chapter unfolds, revealing our fight.

The bonds that are formed, both tender and true,
Carved in the heart, like morning's fresh dew.
Fables of longing, of hope and of trust,
In the tales that we live, in the love that we must.

So gather your stories, let them dance in the air,
Each moment we cherish, a treasure to share.
For in fables of heart, we find who we are,
In the narrative's glow, we shine like a star.

The Echoes of Creativity's Roots

In shadows deep where whispers flow,
Ideas bloom like seeds in snow.
Branches twist, and colors shine,
From fertile ground, the thoughts entwine.

Each heart a canvas, strokes of fate,
Brushes dance, we create our state.
Silent echoes of the past,
Guide the visions that hold fast.

From ancient tales, the sparks ignite,
In realms where passion meets the light.
Through dreams we carve, and kindred souls,
Unlock the mind, let spirit stroll.

In every heartbeat, stories dwell,
A symphony, we weave and tell.
Emanating from our core,
These echoes call for evermore.

So let us paint with thawed resolve,
In art, our mysteries dissolve.
With every brush, we tend the roots,
Wherein the life of creativity shoots.

The Chronicles of Authentic Expression

Pages turn in quiet night,
Voices rise, hearts take flight.
With every word, we bared our skin,
In truth, our journeys thus begin.

Through valleys low and mountains high,
The stories weave, the spirits fly.
Ink and paper, love's embrace,
A testament of space and grace.

In laughter shared and sorrows cried,
Authentic paths where we confide.
Each sentence bold, a vibrant thread,
In this tapestry of what we've said.

Illumined hearts break down the walls,
As every whisper gently calls.
For in the pages of our minds,
The essence of true freedom finds.

We chronicle the life we see,
Transcend the chains, and just be free.
In every line, our souls laid bare,
A journey of profound repair.

A Tidal Wave of Inspiration

Waves crash down, a radiant force,
In every swell, we find our course.
A surge of hope, a call to rise,
Beneath the stars, we claim the skies.

With salt and spray, the world unfolds,
A canvas bright with stories told.
From ocean depths, ideas bloom,
In tempest's heart, we scour the gloom.

Riding currents, swift and free,
Each droplet sparks creativity.
In chaos lies a soothing sound,
Life's symphony reverberates around.

We dive into this endless sea,
In every wave, a harmony.
Casting nets of thoughts afloat,
Inspiration's tide, we gladly quote.

So let us surf the vibrant swells,
In every crest, our spirit dwells.
With hearts ablaze, we welcome grace,
For in this wave, we find our place.

The Confluence of Dreams

Where rivers meet, our visions flow,
In currents bright, new pathways glow.
The confluence whispers tales untold,
A melding pot of dreams so bold.

From distant shores to valleys wide,
In every heart, our hopes collide.
As stars align, we chase the light,
In every dream, the world ignites.

We wander through this sacred land,
With open hearts and steady hand.
In unity, our spirits rise,
Beneath the vast, embracing skies.

With every step, the dreams converse,
In symphony, they break the curse.
Together we pursue our quest,
In this confluence, we are blessed.

So let the rivers guide our way,
In harmony, we choose to stay.
For in this journey, hand in hand,
The confluence of dreams shall stand.

The Spark of Innovation

In the stillness, ideas ignite,
A whisper of dreams taking flight.
Bright minds collide, wisdom flows,
Creating new paths where wonder grows.

Curiosity fuels the flame,
Every thought a potential name.
With passion and purpose, we strive,
To transform the world, keep hopes alive.

From sketches to plans, the journey starts,
In every setback, resilience imparts.
A tapestry woven with daring threads,
Crafting the future with courage and leads.

In the chaos, a symphony found,
Innovation's pulse, a vibrant sound.
With every failure, we learn and rise,
Unfolding our dreams beneath open skies.

Together we stand, a united force,
Navigating the waves, we chart our course.
The spark of creation, a guiding light,
Illuminating paths in darkest night.

A Journey Within

In silence, we wander, we seek,
Exploring the depths, the strong and the weak.
Through valleys of doubt, we must roam,
Finding the courage to make it home.

Reflections emerge, like whispers so clear,
Echoing truths we hold dear.
With every breath, we pause and feel,
The weight of our stories, the strength to heal.

Time bends as we search through the haze,
In labyrinths of thought, we daze.
Unearthing gems beneath the noise,
Rediscovering hope, reclaiming our joys.

Each moment a lesson, each path a guide,
Navigating the currents, we won't hide.
With mindful steps, in this inner quest,
We uncover the self that knows best.

In the embrace of shadows, light we'll find,
Awakening dreams that linger behind.
A journey within, an endless tie,
To the heartbeat of life, we reach for the sky.

Breathing Life into Words

A page awaits, blank and bright,
Holding whispers, ready for flight.
With every stroke, a pulse creates,
Breathing life into written fates.

In ink we find our deepest fears,
Pouring out truths, watering tears.
Stories woven with love and pain,
Capturing moments like drops of rain.

Each word a brush, painting the scene,
Expressing the silent, the unheard dream.
Through prose and verse, we ignite hearts,
Transforming thoughts into sacred arts.

The rhythm of language, soft and tight,
Guiding us through the dark of night.
In verses, we float, in stanzas, we dive,
Finding a pulse that keeps us alive.

Breathing life into words, a dance unfolds,
A journey of stories yet to be told.
In every letter, a world we find,
Connecting us all, heart intertwined.

The Art of Unfolding

Like petals that bloom in the sun,
Life gently teaches, we learn to run.
Through twists and turns, we embrace the sway,
The art of unfolding in every way.

Moments reveal what was hidden within,
Exposing the layers, where dreams begin.
Step by step, as the journey unfolds,
We gather the courage to be bold.

In the pages of time, each chapter we claim,
A story of growth, never the same.
With grace we discover, through joy and through strife,
The beauty of change, the essence of life.

Wounds may teach us the softest of grace,
Heartbeats align as we find our place.
With every experience, wisdom is born,
In the delicate dance of our lives adorned.

Unfolding like origami in air,
Each crease a reminder, of love and care.
As we open our hearts, we begin to see,
The art of unfolding, eternally free.

Dancing with Ideas

In the realm where thoughts do twirl,
Minds set free in a vibrant whirl.
Each notion spins, a joyful flight,
Glimmers of hope in the dancing light.

Whispers of dreams sway in the air,
Embracing passion, vibrant and rare.
With every step, the rhythms grow,
As inspiration begins to flow.

They leap and sway in boundless glee,
Painting visions for the world to see.
A fest of colors, ideas unite,
A beautiful dance, pure and bright.

Twisting and turning, the dance unfolds,
In the heart of creation, stories told.
Through swirling thoughts, they find their way,
In the laughter of night and the blush of day.

So let us dance, with ideas alive,
In this vivid space where dreams can thrive.
For in each twist, we find what's new,
Embracing the magic of the untrue.

Light in the Creative Shadows

In corners dark, ideas hide,
Flickers of light, the creators' guide.
Shadows dance, where whispers ring,
The glow of insight leads to spring.

Through muted shades, the colors play,
Unseen brilliance ready to sway.
Artistry blooms in the dusky glow,
As visions rise, preparing to flow.

Each shadow holds a tale to spin,
A canvas vast where we begin.
Beneath the surface, treasures lie,
Waiting for mind's eye to pry.

So trust the dark, it fuels the flame,
Where hidden thoughts carve out a name.
Let the light in and shadows blend,
Creating pathways that never end.

In this dance of light and dark,
The soul ignites the final spark.
And out of shadows, dreams take flight,
Guided by our inner light.

The Alchemy of Vision

In the forge of imagination bright,
Ideas are mixed in the heart of night.
Transforming thoughts to visions bold,
In alchemy's grasp, new futures unfold.

With every spark, potential glows,
As dreams converge, the magic flows.
Casting hopes in a molten stream,
Creating life from a fleeting dream.

The quest unfolds through trials faced,
With every twist, new paths embraced.
In the crucible of fire and stone,
Ideas meld, creating the unknown.

The alchemist's touch, a sacred art,
Turning the mundane to something smart.
Through vision's lens, we start to see,
The endless wonders of what can be.

So let the elements guide our quest,
In the alchemy of dreams, we find our zest.
From thought to form, the journey's true,
With every heartbeat, we start anew.

Paths of the Inventive Mind

Through winding trails, the thinkers roam,
In inventive worlds they carve a home.
Exploring ideas, where few have tread,
Unraveling threads, where dreams are led.

Each step forward ignites a spark,
Illuminating all that's dark.
Pioneers of thought, brave and bold,
Crafting futures that can't be controlled.

With every question, a door swings wide,
Inviting new paths where insights abide.
Together they wander, hearts in tune,
Creating wonders, under the moon.

In the tapestry of minds intertwined,
Weaving visions that seek to find.
Inventive whispers guide the way,
Opening portals to a brighter day.

So let us cherish this journey grand,
As we walk together, hand in hand.
For the paths we create, each twist and bind,
Shape the essence of the inventive mind.

The Fabric of Ingenuity

Threads of thought entwine in light,
Weavers dance through day and night.
Ideas spark, igniting fire,
Crafting dreams that never tire.

Colors blend, a vibrant scheme,
Sewing futures, bold and keen.
Stitch by stitch, the patterns grow,
In the loom, creativity flows.

Gears turn in minds that dare,
Inventing wonders from thin air.
Blueprints drawn, hope's design,
Innovation's touch is divine.

In the fabric, stories dwell,
Every patch a tale to tell.
Glimmers of genius, a bright thread,
Weaving paths where hearts are led.

Through the fabric, worlds align,
Crafted visions intertwine.
In each seam, the genius lies,
Crafting futures, bold and wise.

Labyrinths of Fantasy

In the maze where dreams reside,
Magic whispers, secrets hide.
Winding paths twist and turn,
In the heart, the fire burns.

Starry skies ignite the night,
Guiding souls by shimmering light.
Imagination takes its flight,
In this realm, all feels right.

Creatures dance, with tales to weave,
Lost in dreams, we dare believe.
Every corner holds delight,
In labyrinths, pure and bright.

Echoes call from distant lands,
Crafting worlds with gentle hands.
Mysteries await the bold,
Within these walls, the brave unfold.

Journey deep, let shadows play,
Follow where your heart may sway.
In the labyrinth, magic finds,
Endless wonders for the minds.

Awakening the Muse

In the stillness, whispers call,
Beneath the stars, a silent thrall.
Hearts awakened, spirits rise,
Through the darkness, beauty flies.

Gentle breeze stirs dormant dreams,
Flowing softly, sweet moonbeams.
Inspiration blooms like flowers,
Awakening through quiet hours.

Ink spills forth, a vibrant stream,
With each stroke, we dare to dream.
Voices echo in the night,
Muses dance, igniting light.

From the ashes, hope takes flight,
In the dawn, we chase the light.
Creating art with every breath,
From this moment, no more death.

Awakening, the world we see,
Boundless realms of creativity.
Let your heart sing loud and true,
The muse awaits, just for you.

Chronicles of the Inspired Heart

In pages worn, tales unfold,
Stories whispered, dreams retold.
Each heartbeat, a rhythm of grace,
Chronicles etch in time and space.

Words like rivers flow with ease,
Crafting moments, memories tease.
In every line, a part of soul,
The inspired heart, forever whole.

Gathered voices, strong and clear,
In these chronicles, we persevere.
Through trials faced, we find our way,
With courage sought, come what may.

Ink-stained fingers tell the truth,
Retelling joys and tales of youth.
In the depths, hope's ember glows,
In this journey, love bestows.

United pages, woven tight,
Each story spark ignites the night.
In the chronicles, hearts align,
Together we rise, forever shine.

Horizons of New Ideas

A spark ignites within the mind,
Dreams take flight, new paths we find.
Visions bright, they dance and swirl,
In the heart, possibilities unfurl.

With every thought, a step we take,
Beyond the shores, we start to make.
New dawns rise, the future gleams,
Crafting life from vibrant dreams.

Each soul a voice, a unique role,
In the symphony, we play as whole.
Together we craft what's yet to see,
Like branches of a mighty tree.

Ideas bloom like flowers rare,
In gardens nurtured with tender care.
The winds of change, they softly blow,
Guiding seeds that we will sow.

Horizons stretch, the journey's wide,
Innovation waits, let's turn the tide.
Embrace the new, let passion lead,
In unity, we plant the seed.

The Canvas of Endless Possibilities

Brush strokes bold on a canvas white,
Colors swirl in joyous flight.
Each hue a thought, each line a dream,
In this world, we craft the scheme.

Palette rich, with shades that blend,
Imagination knows no end.
With every stroke, our visions bloom,
Transforming blank space into room.

Textures speak of tales untold,
Within this frame, our hearts unfold.
We paint the future, bright and clear,
A masterpiece we hold so dear.

Every journey starts with a line,
Contours shifting, designs divine.
In this space, we redefine,
Life's grand story, yours and mine.

Embrace the mess, let chaos reign,
For in the wild, creativity gains.
On this canvas, we'll strive and play,
Creating magic every day.

The Choreography of Imagination

In the silence, thoughts pirouette,
Each idea, a dancer, deftly set.
They leap and twirl in radiant grace,
Creating rhythms in time and space.

Like music notes, they intertwine,
Crafting patterns so divine.
Every movement tells a tale,
In this ballet, we cannot fail.

With every breath, we catch the light,
In this dance, our spirits ignite.
Exploring worlds where dreams reside,
In the heart, our visions guide.

The stage is set, the curtains rise,
Through leaps of faith, we touch the skies.
Imagination leads the way,
In this choreography, we sway.

With passion's fire, we take our stand,
Together, unified, hand in hand.
We celebrate the art of creation,
In this dance of inspiration.

Whirls of Innovative Spirit

A tempest brews within the soul,
Ideas spin like a swirling goal.
In the vortex, thoughts collide,
Where imagination cannot hide.

Visions burst like stars at night,
Illuminating paths with light.
Creative minds, forever free,
Explore the depths of what can be.

In this whirl, we find our pace,
Daring to dream, we embrace the chase.
Every twist, each turn a chance,
To shape our lives, to find our dance.

With every gust, new dreams arise,
A tapestry woven in vibrant skies.
No boundaries hold us, we take the leap,
In the whirls, our visions seep.

Let this spirit soar and sing,
For from our hearts, great wonders spring.
In the whirlwind's embrace, we ignite,
A journey shared, in pure delight.

The Dance of Inventive Whispers

In shadows soft, ideas twirl,
A melody of thoughts unfurl.
Each whisper spins, a tale untold,
Creativity's embrace, bold.

Colors blend in a quiet haze,
As minds ignite in a playful blaze.
Together they weave a vibrant thread,
In the realm where concepts tread.

Secrets linger among the light,
In every corner, hidden insight.
With gentle hands, we craft and mold,
A world born anew, bright and bold.

Each flicker brings a spark anew,
Bound together, old and new.
Innovations in the air, alive,
Where inventive spirits thrive.

So let the dance of whispers play,
In every heart, they find their way.
Through silent nights and vibrant days,
Creativity's eternal praise.

Beneath the Veil of Fantasy

In twilight realms where dreams take flight,
A shroud of stars adorns the night.
Whispers echo from distant lands,
Where magic blooms in gentle strands.

Beneath the veil, the secrets grow,
In gardens where wild wishes flow.
Each petal holds a tale so bright,
A dance of shadows, pure delight.

The lanterns glow with a mystic gleam,
Inviting hearts to dare and dream.
With every step, a story spins,
A tapestry where wonder begins.

The moonlight bathes all in silver grace,
In this enchanted, timeless space.
The air is thick with hopes and sighs,
As fantasy in sweet silence lies.

So close your eyes and take a chance,
In the realm where wishes dance.
Beneath the veil, let spirits soar,
Finding magic forevermore.

Mosaic of Insights

In every shard, a vision gleams,
Pieces gathered from fleeting dreams.
A tapestry of thoughts combined,
In the heart where wisdom's blind.

Colors clash in a vibrant array,
Each insight found along the way.
Fragments tell of sorrow and joy,
In a mosaic none can destroy.

With careful hands, we shape the whole,
A masterpiece for every soul.
Each moment captured, rich and true,
Crafting life from shades of hue.

In silence deep, reflections grow,
Along the path where seekers go.
A glance unveiled, a truth will show,
In a world that's ever aglow.

So gather pieces, don't despair,
In the mosaic, we all share.
Bringing harmony into the light,
Together, we make the future bright.

Celestial Sparks

Amidst the stars, a flicker glows,
A dance of light where love bestows.
Each spark ignites the velvet skies,
A symphony where wonder lies.

Galaxies swirl in cosmic grace,
Embracing time in endless space.
With every twinkle, dreams ignite,
A canvas painted through the night.

Comets streak and memories fade,
In stardust paths, a dance is made.
Together we soar, hearts ablaze,
In this celestial, timeless phase.

The universe whispers tales of old,
Of journeys vast and brave, bold.
With every heartbeat, we can find,
The spark that lights the soul and mind.

So let your wishes ride the streams,
In this expanse where magic beams.
For in the night, we're all aligned,
Celestial sparks that we might bind.

Vines of Vision

Twisting leaves in bright sunlight,
Whispering secrets of the night.
Roots buried deep in olden ground,
A tapestry of life unbound.

Branching out like thoughts in flight,
Each moment clear, a moment slight.
Tangled paths where dreams entwine,
Spirited visions that softly shine.

Nature's brush paints vivid scenes,
Woven tales in emerald greens.
With every breeze, new winds arise,
A gentle dance 'neath endless skies.

In shadows cast by twilight's glow,
The stories of the vines we know.
Adventures call through rustling leaves,
A world alive, where spirit weaves.

Life's adventure, boundless, free,
In the heart of each old tree.
With every vine that climbs and grows,
A universe of dreams bestows.

A Symphony of Silence

In the quiet of the night,
Stars begin their whispering flight.
Moonlit shadows softly sway,
In gentle calm, hearts drift away.

The stillness hums a melody,
Composed of every memory.
Each pause, a note in time's embrace,
A symphony of inner space.

Echoes of what once was near,
Softly murmur, crystal clear.
Restless thoughts find solace here,
In the silence, dreams draw near.

Waves of peace, a soothing balm,
In hushed tones, the world feels calm.
The heart's rhythm, slow and true,
In the quiet, life renews.

A sacred space where spirits roam,
Finding shelter, finding home.
In stillness, every soul can see,
The beauty born of silence free.

The Color Palette of Dreams

Brushstrokes of twilight kiss the dawn,
Hues of hope in a world reborn.
Whirlwinds of thoughts, vivid and bright,
A canvas alive with pure delight.

Lavender skies whisper sweet dreams,
Rippling streams reflect moonbeams.
Every shade a story told,
In every corner, wonders unfold.

Crimson sunsets, fierce and bold,
Golden rays of warmth extolled.
A palette rich, a vibrant scene,
Awakening the soul's unseen.

From sapphire depths of the ocean wide,
Emerald fields, where dreams abide.
With every brush, a heart's desire,
Igniting passion, setting fire.

In hues of laughter, shades of tears,
Each color carries hopes and fears.
An artist's touch, serene and pure,
In dreams, true magic can endure.

Sowing Seeds of Imagination

In the garden of the mind,
New ideas spring forth, unconfined.
Planting hopes in fertile ground,
With every thought, new worlds are found.

Tiny seeds take root and grow,
Emerging visions, bright as glow.
Tending dreams with gentle care,
Nurtured well, they flourish there.

From whispers soft to shouts of joy,
Imagination, a wondrous toy.
Cultivating thoughts that dance and play,
In sunlight's warmth, they'll find their way.

Harvesting wonders, rich and rare,
A bounteous yield beyond compare.
With every bloom, new paths appear,
In the garden, hearts draw near.

So sow the seeds, let visions spring,
Each vibrant dream a song to sing.
In the tapestry of thought's embrace,
Imagination finds its place.

The Echo Chamber of Visionaries

In a room filled with dreams, the whispers grow,
Bright thoughts collide, igniting a glow.
Voices of hope float on the air,
Ideas exchanged with a fervent care.

Shadows dance, revealing the light,
Courage blooms in the depth of the night.
Blueprints of futures written in stars,
Together we shatter our inner bars.

Notes of chaos turn into song,
Each heartbeat echoes where we belong.
Chasing the echoes, we find our way,
Creating new paths, brightening the grey.

Bridges of thoughts, so unafraid,
Underneath doubts, convictions are laid.
In the echo chamber, visions take flight,
Carving our names in the fabric of night.

With eyes unbound, we venture near,
In the glow of hope, we conquer fear.
For in this space, visions align,
Together we weave the grand design.

Capturing Lightning in a Jar

Moments of brilliance flash in our mind,
Whispers of wonder, fleeting yet kind.
With open hearts, we reach for the spark,
Chasing the light through shadows so dark.

In the stillness, we find our muse,
A lightning bolt dances, refusing to lose.
Embrace the storm, let the thunder roll,
Capture the essence that makes us whole.

Threads of creation we weave with delight,
Stitches of passion, a tapestry bright.
Each flicker preserved, a memory dear,
In the jar of our dreams, we hold our fear.

Nature's wild energy flows through our hands,
Transforming the chaos into radiant strands.
In every flicker, a promise we chase,
For lightning contained is a testament of grace.

So gather your courage, unleash the spark,
For in every heart lies a light in the dark.
Let the jar glow with the fire of our will,
A beacon of hope, inspiring us still.

The Journal of Reflections

Pages turn softly, whispering fate,
Ink flows like rivers, thoughts resonate.
Worn edges tell stories, time unfolds,
Secrets of heartbeats, visions retold.

Within each line, a moment captured,
Emotions unveiled, the noise silenced.
With every stroke, a piece of the soul,
Sharing the journey of becoming whole.

A mirror of dreams, both shattered and bright,
Lessons of love penned by candlelight.
Rivers of memory flow through the pen,
Reflecting the past, yet beckoning again.

In quiet reflections, we find our truth,
Waking the echoes of playful youth.
As ink spills dreams, we dare to believe,
In the power of words, we find reprieve.

Close the journal, hold it tight,
A chronicle of shadows, a dance of light.
In every reflection, we craft our lore,
A journey of whispers forevermore.

Blooming Ideas in Silent Spaces

In the hush of the dawn, creativity brews,
Gentle thoughts blossom, as daylight renews.
Petals of wisdom unfurl with the sun,
In silent spaces, great journeys begun.

Amidst the stillness, we listen and grow,
Ideas take root, where the soft breezes blow.
Whispers of dreaming, a soft lullaby,
In the quiet embrace, we dare to fly.

Sown seeds of passion in fertile ground,
Each silent moment a treasure profound.
From silence emerges a beautiful thought,
In sacred silence, our battles are fought.

Colors of thought merge in serene glow,
In the heart of stillness, our visions flow.
As echoes retreat, new pathways ignite,
In blooming ideas, we find our light.

So cherish the quiet, let the silence speak,
For in open spaces, it's growth that we seek.
With minds unshackled, we rise and embrace,
The beauty of silence, our wondrous place.

The Bloom of Wild Concepts

Ideas sprout in vivid hues,
Each thought a petal, bright as news.
In the garden of the mind, they dance,
Unfurling dreams with every glance.

Winds of change begin to blow,
Whispers of where the wild thoughts go.
Nature's script, in colors bold,
Stories of wonders yet untold.

Seeds of wisdom take their flight,
Transforming darkness into light.
In wild concepts, freedom reigns,
The heart spills joy and lets it reign.

Beneath the sky, a canvas wide,
Uncharted paths where thoughts confide.
Each bloom a chance to redefine,
In every petal, paths entwine.

So let them grow, these wild ideas,
Nurtured deep with hopes and cheers.
For in this garden, dreams align,
And every thought is pure divine.

Reflections in a Creative Pool

In quiet waters, visions flow,
Mirrored thoughts, soft and slow.
Ripples form with every spark,
Lighting up the quiet dark.

Brushstrokes dance on liquid glass,
Colors blend as moments pass.
Each wave a chance to dive and swim,
To find the truth in shadows dim.

Echoes linger, fading bright,
In the stillness, dreams take flight.
The pool reflects the mood we share,
Creative whispers linger there.

Each ripple tells a story true,
Unlocking paths within the blue.
Emotions swirl, a vibrant hue,
Creating worlds that feel anew.

So gaze upon this sacred space,
Where art and soul find their place.
The creative pool, a wondrous sight,
Uplifting hearts, igniting light.

Imprints of the Soul

Footprints left on timeless sand,
Each step a story, softly planned.
In the warmth of the sun's embrace,
Echoes linger in this place.

Whispers of laughter fill the air,
Moments cherished, spun with care.
The tide of time, it ebbs and flows,
Washing dreams where the heart grows.

In the depths of quiet night,
Imprints shine like stars so bright.
Each memory a luminous trace,
Binding past within this space.

Through the storms and sunshine's glow,
The soul's imprints weave and flow.
Marking paths we dare to tread,
The story of life is never shed.

So honor these steps, both meek and grand,
For they create the life we planned.
In every imprint, love's embrace,
A journey painted with grace.

The Architecture of Dreams

In twilight skies, the towers rise,
Crafted from hope and spun from skies.
Each brick a wish, each beam a thought,
In the mind's eye, the true is caught.

Winding roads through realms unknown,
This blueprint carved from hearts alone.
Sketches drawn in starlit space,
Building visions with gentle grace.

Windows wide to the cosmic view,
Where each reflection tells of you.
The frames of trust, the walls of love,
A sanctuary from above.

Columns strong of memories made,
In every corner, dreams are laid.
The roof of clouds, where hopes soar high,
Embracing whispers of the sky.

So let us dwell in this fine design,
A world of dreams that's truly mine.
In the architecture, hearts convene,
Creating life, a vivid scene.

The Echo Chamber of Ideas

In halls of thought, echoes roam,
Whispers of dreams, seeds to comb.
Voices collide, they twist and turn,
In the heart of silence, passions burn.

Reflections dance on walls of mind,
Waves of wonder, uniquely entwined.
Questions that linger, answers take flight,
In this chamber, we seek the light.

Minds like prisms, casting their beams,
Filtering visions, igniting our dreams.
Each voice a thread in a vibrant loom,
Together we rise, amidst the gloom.

Ideas cascade like a river wide,
Through currents of thought, let's take a ride.
In echoes we trust, as visions expand,
Hand in hand, we'll make our stand.

So let us gather, let hearts combine,
In this echo chamber, let us shine.
Building a world where thoughts align,
Join the chorus, let voices entwine.

Threads of Invention

Woven from dreams and sparks of desire,
Threads of thought, igniting a fire.
Patterns of progress, stitched with care,
In the fabric of time, we're destined to share.

Ideas unfold like petals in spring,
Each one unique, a magical thing.
With hands that create, we paint the night,
In the loom of our minds, we find the light.

In the workshop of life, tools in our grip,
We carve our visions, let creativity slip.
Inventing a future from fibers of hope,
With threads of connection, we learn how to cope.

Echoes of laughter, melodies hum,
Inventions that dance like beat of a drum.
Around every corner, a spark to ignite,
Tapestries woven with passion and might.

So gather your threads, let visions unite,
In the loom of invention, we'll shine so bright.
Creating a world where dreams intertwine,
Through threads of invention, our fates align.

Flickers of Ingenuity

In the shadow of night, a spark appears,
Flickers of genius, calming our fears.
Bright ideas dance on a canvas unseen,
Each brushstroke a whisper, where dreams convene.

Twists of the mind, like rivers they flow,
Navigating paths where no one can go.
Moments of clarity sharpening sight,
Flickers of ingenuity, igniting the night.

In silence we ponder, in chaos we weave,
Crafting the stories that we dare believe.
Visions once hidden, now take the stage,
Ignited by spirit, let's turn the page.

From fragments of thought, a tapestry grows,
Innovative winds through the garden it sows.
Each flicker a promise, like stars in the sky,
In the realm of creation, together we'll fly.

So let us embrace the sparks that we find,
Celebrate ingenuity, the brilliance of mind.
With each flicker of light, let imagination steer,
In a world of wonder, we'll conquer our fear.

The Picture-Book of Emotions

Pages unfold with colors so bright,
Capturing moments, in day and in night.
Each chapter a feeling, a story to tell,
In the picture-book of emotions, we dwell.

Joy is a sunrise, painted in gold,
While sorrow flows soft, like stories of old.
With laughter like rainbows, we dance in delight,
Collecting the hues of our shared human plight.

Fear is a shadow, lurking nearby,
Yet courage ignites, like a dove in the sky.
Hope is a whisper, a soft gentle breeze,
That carries our dreams on the crest of the seas.

Anger burns bright, a flickering flame,
Yet in its reflection, we find our true name.
Emotions like paintings, each one a new brush,
In the gallery of life, we're caught in the rush.

So let's leaf through the pages, explore what we feel,
In the picture-book of emotions, let's heal.
Each illustration tells the tale of our heart,
In this book of connections, we all play a part.

Whispers of the Heart's Artistry

In shadows soft, our secrets dwell,
With colors bright, our stories swell.
Each stroke of love, a silent song,
In whispered dreams, where we belong.

The canvas waits, for strokes to start,
With every shade, we pour our heart.
Emotions blend in vivid hue,
A masterpiece, just me and you.

In fleeting moments, passions rise,
Through painted skies, where silence lies.
Each brush, a tale that comes alive,
In heart's embrace, our spirits thrive.

Crafting worlds from mere desire,
With tender hands, we build a pyre.
The flicker glows, igniting spark,
In artistry, we leave our mark.

So let us dance on this fine thread,
Of dreams and hopes, where love is fed.
In whispers soft, our hearts convey,
The artistry of love's ballet.

The Voyage of Ideas

On waves of thought, we set our sail,
In search of truths, where minds prevail.
Across the seas of endless quest,
We journey forth, our dreams possess.

Each thought a star, in night's embrace,
Guiding us through this boundless space.
With every wave, new visions grow,
In currents strong, where passions flow.

Together we chart uncharted lands,
With open hearts and willing hands.
Innovation blooms on every shore,
As ideas like treasures, we explore.

Through storms and calm, we dance along,
With courage fierce, we sing our song.
Each revelation, a guiding light,
In this grand voyage, we take flight.

So let us sail 'neath starry skies,
With dreams anew, and brighter ties.
A journey bold, forever grand,
The voyage of ideas, hand in hand.

The Lightbulb Moment

In shadows deep, a spark ignites,
A sudden thought that shifts our sights.
When clarity breaks through the night,
The world transforms, bathed in light.

Like lightning striking, fresh and new,
A burst of insight breaks right through.
In simple things, the complex gleams,
Awakening our wildest dreams.

The gears engage, the mind afire,
Illuminating every desire.
What once seemed lost now finds a way,
With newfound hope, we seize the day.

In that brief flash, all falls in place,
Connections made, a warm embrace.
Ideas swirl in vibrant dance,
The lightbulb moment leads our chance.

So cherish these sparks, let them grow,
For in their glow, we learn and know.
With every flicker, life can bloom,
In light's embrace, dispelling gloom.

The Fertile Plains of the Mind

In quiet lands where thoughts reside,
The fertile fields of dreams abide.
With seeds of wisdom, we take root,
In gardens lush, ambition's fruit.

Ideas sprout where waters flow,
In sunlight's beam, new visions grow.
Each concept nurtured, blooms so bright,
Transforming earth to pure delight.

From barren thoughts to fertile ground,
In rich terrain, our hopes are found.
With every rain, the spirit thrives,
In this expanse, the heart contrives.

So let us plow the fields of mind,
In search of treasures yet to find.
With every step, we cultivate,
In this vast land, we create fate.

The fertile plains await our hand,
With love and trust, we understand.
In endless growth, our dreams do climb,
The boundless scope of space and time.

Stories in the Shadows

In the night when silence speaks,
Whispers weave through ancient trees,
Hidden tales begin to creep,
Echoing beneath the leaves.

Flickering lights dance in the dark,
Dreams and fears in shadows play,
Ghostly figures leave their mark,
Woven threads of yesterday.

Every corner holds a secret,
Every path a tale untold,
Darkened places whisper sweetly,
Mysteries in shades of gold.

Footsteps linger, memories fade,
In the depth of twilight's breath,
Stories linger, slowly made,
In the heart, they rise from death.

The night unfolds its velvet cloak,
Revealing truths in spectral light,
In the shadows, words are woke,
Life and death, a dance of night.

Moonlight on a Blank Page

Underneath the silver glow,
A canvas waits, untouched, serene,
Thoughts like rivers gently flow,
Words unspoken yet unseen.

A quill poised in quiet grace,
Ink ready to embrace the night,
Emotions rise, a soft embrace,
As shadows blend with silvery light.

Each stroke a vision, bold and bright,
A story starts to take its shape,
Dreams emerge from endless night,
With every line, new worlds escape.

Moonlight glimmers, soft and true,
Casting secrets on the page,
In this moment, old and new,
Dreams and stories intergage.

As dawn arrives, the page reveals,
A universe crafted with care,
Moonlight fades, but spirit heals,
In every word, the night laid bare.

The Rhythm of Creation

In the heart where echoes thrive,
Beats of life begin to swell,
Nature wakes, feels alive,
In every pulse, a sacred spell.

Stars aligned in cosmic dance,
Galaxies swirl in swirling hue,
From chaos springs a newfound chance,
A world reborn, fresh and true.

Rhythms rise and fall like tides,
Breath of wind, and whispers call,
In the cycle, wonder bides,
Creation's song enchants us all.

Every beat a tender birth,
Rippling through the fabric tight,
From the depths of ocean's girth,
To the heights of stars' white light.

In this dance of time and fate,
Echoes linger, soft and light,
The rhythm calls, we hesitate,
Yet in the pulse, we find our flight.

Wings of Possibility

In the dawn where hope takes flight,
Dreams unfurl with vibrant hue,
Every moment feels so right,
Carrying whispers of the new.

Wings of courage lift us high,
Beyond the bounds of what we know,
In the heart, a fiery sky,
A spark ignites, begins to grow.

With each breath, we dare to soar,
Across the realms of what could be,
Infinite paths call us to explore,
In every choice, a journey free.

Nestled in the strength of chance,
We find our voices, bold and clear,
The world awaits our painted dance,
As we embrace what we hold dear.

So let us spread these wings so wide,
In unity, we seek the sky,
With every step, we choose the ride,
To touch the stars as we fly high.

Rivers of the Unconventional

In whispers flow the hidden streams,
Carving paths where others dream.
Veering off the tired route,
They dance and twist, no need to suit.

A spark ignites in murky depths,
Where silence breathes and secrets heft.
Unraveled tales on splashing banks,
A chorus sings without the ranks.

Their currents merge, a bold embrace,
With laughter laced through each bold trace.
A tapestry of minds set free,
They weave the fabric of what could be.

In rugged beds they find their face,
Reflecting dreams, a sacred space.
Beyond the shouts of crowd and noise,
These rivers flow with quiet joys.

Each bend reveals a new delight,
Where shadows play with morning light.
And in the depths of wild unknown,
The unconventional finds its throne.

Kaleidoscope of Vision

Through shards of color, worlds collide,
Visions dance and twist with pride.
A fractured lens of radiant hue,
Reflecting dreams both bright and true.

In every turn a tale unfolds,
Of scattered moments, brave and bold.
Perspectives shift like quickened time,
In patterns found within the rhyme.

From chaos blooms a fleeting scene,
Where past and future intertwine, serene.
A symphony of sight and sound,
In kaleidoscopes, lost and found.

The swirling forms begin to blend,
In every fragment, life transcends.
With every gaze, new stories spark,
Illuminating shadows stark.

So let the colors lead the way,
Embrace the visions born of play.
For in this dance of shapes we see,
The endless realms of possibility.

The Spirit of the Unwritten

In empty pages, silence speaks,
A voice that whispers, never weak.
The ink may flow, but fate remains,
A dance of ideas in quiet chains.

The stories wait, their breath held tight,
In shadows cloaked from human sight.
Each word a seed, in stillness sown,
A yearning heart finds hope alone.

An echo stirs, a dream awakes,
Inking pathways through the aches.
The spirit calls from realms abodes,
Awakening thoughts like winding roads.

Through time and space, the tales await,
In every heart, in every fate.
So dare to chart what lies ahead,
In pages blank, where fears are shed.

The unwritten holds a sacred trust,
A canvas vast, a cosmic gust.
With every breath, let poems flow,
In whispered dreams, let stories grow.

Spheres of Freethought

In circles spun, ideas drift,
A dance of thoughts, a gentle lift.
Where boundaries fade and borders break,
In open minds, new visions wake.

Through spheres that blend, perspectives shift,
In every round, a precious gift.
A tapestry of voices shared,
In harmony, we're gently bared.

No walls can cage the soaring mind,
In freedom's grasp, new truths we find.
Each notion sparks a vibrant flame,
In spheres of thought, we lose the tame.

Beyond the norm, where shadows dwell,
We wander forth, we break the spell.
With every idea, we grow and spread,
In realms of thought, where dreams are fed.

So let us gather, hand in hand,
In open circles, we will stand.
For in these spheres, we dare proclaim,
That every thought can forge a name.

Luminescent Pathways

Beneath the stars, a trail unfolds,
Soft glimmers of hope, stories told.
Each step a dance on the edge of night,
Illuminated dreams take joyous flight.

Lanterns of laughter guide the way,
Casting shadows where doubts betray.
In the glow of courage, fears dissolve,
Emerging paths that together resolve.

Whispers of starlight in gentle breeze,
Leading us onward with effortless ease.
Echoes of journeys etched in the ground,
In these luminescent pathways, we're found.

With every heartbeat, a spark ignites,
Shining bright, forever in sight.
Navigating through the forest of time,
Finding the rhythm, a celestial rhyme.

Hand in hand with the cosmos we tread,
In the warm glow of dreams overhead.
Following pathways that shimmer and sway,
Together we wander, come what may.

Unfolding the Unknown

In the hush before dawn, possibilities rise,
Veils of the future softly disguise.
Curiosity whispers, urging a chase,
As mysteries beckon with delicate grace.

Each moment a chapter waiting to tell,
Stories half-seen in a enchanting spell.
Unraveling secrets as day breaks anew,
In the fabric of time, threads woven true.

Footprints of wonder in uncharted ground,
Echoes of choices that linger around.
With hearts wide open, we step into dream,
Embracing the chaos, a vibrant stream.

In storms of uncertainty, beauty can bloom,
In shadows of doubt, the light finds room.
Together we wander, unhindered by fear,
The unknown our canvas, the future is near.

With each heartbeat, new pathways arise,
Transforming the dusk into brilliant skies.
Unfolding the unknown, hand in hand we go,
Chasing the horizons where possibilities flow.

The Pulse of Originality

In the rhythm of life, a heartbeat of soul,
Echoes of passion that make us whole.
Every heartbeat a dance, bold and divine,
Breathing in brilliance, a unique design.

Colors of creativity splash on the page,
In the gallery of thoughts, we break free from cage.
Fleeting ideas can spark like a flame,
In the pulse of originality, we reclaim our name.

Every device, a tool for the brave,
Crafting the visions that our spirits crave.
With open minds, we celebrate grace,
In the melody of being, we find our place.

From the depths of silence, a symphony swells,
Echoes of truth that resonate spells.
Through the creative maze, we joyfully roam,
In the pulse of originality, we find our home.

Dance with the universe, let ideas flow,
In this vibrant cosmos, we endlessly glow.
The world a canvas, painted by hands,
The pulse of originality, where beauty expands.

Colors of the Mind's Canvas

Brushstrokes of emerald dreams,
Swirling in a vivid light,
Brush, in rhythm, it redeems,
Creating scenes, a pure delight.

Crimson whispers, secrets told,
On the palette of the heart,
Golden hues, a warmth of gold,
Where imagination finds its art.

Azure tides of thought cascade,
Flowing through the years unseen,
Pastel shadows danced and played,
In the depths of what has been.

Violet visions hover near,
Shapes and forms in twilight fade,
Every color holds a cheer,
In the vibrant dreams we've made.

Each stroke a piece of our soul,
A reflection in vivid streams,
Together we create a whole,
In the colors of our dreams.

Embroidery of Thought

Threads of color weave through dreams,
Tapestries of ideas bursting at seams.
Soft whispers of wisdom stitch the night,
In patterns of shadows, glimpses of light.

Each stitch a story, each knot a plan,
Fingers dance gently, guiding the span.
Intricate visions in silence unfurl,
Spinning the fabric of this vast world.

In moments of stillness, creativity flows,
Dancing through fibers where imagination grows.
Yarns of connection, soft and profound,
In the heart of the weaver, magic is found.

Crafting the future with delicate care,
Embroidered memories floating in air.
Seeking the essence in threads intertwined,
In the art of our thoughts, true treasure we find.

With each heartbeat, new colors arise,
The canvas of being, a grand surprise.
In layers of meaning, we search for our place,
Embroidery of thought, a timeless embrace.

The Symphony of Whimsy

Notes of laughter fill the air,
Dancing through the day so bright,
Wishes twirling everywhere,
In a melody of pure delight.

Chimes of joy in playful beat,
Echoes of imagination,
Rhythms of life, both light and sweet,
Creating joyous celebration.

Flutes of fancy, flaring high,
In the garden of delight,
Strings of yearning float and fly,
Painting every thought in light.

A cosmic orchestra awakes,
Each heart a note, each dream a song,
Together strumming, no mistakes,
In this symphony we belong.

Harmonies of joy resound,
In whimsical tunes, we find,
Every laugh a magic sound,
In the symphony of mind.

Constellations of Possibility

Stars that twinkle, bright and bold,
Every glance a chance to see,
Stories of dreams yet untold,
In the night sky, wild and free.

Galaxies of thought reside,
In the cosmos of our souls,
Traveling paths where hopes abide,
Illuminating endless goals.

Nebulas form in brilliant hues,
Waves of wonder wash ashore,
Every spark a chance to choose,
In the heavens, we explore.

Orbits twist, and futures gleam,
Every moment holds a chance,
In the fabric of a dream,
Where reality can dance.

Comets blaze with fleeting grace,
In the dark, our wishes soar,
Guided by the starlit space,
To constellations, we will door.

The Playground of Ideas

In the sandbox of our minds,
Thoughts are molded, shaped with care,
Building castles, art that binds,
With imagination everywhere.

Slides of laughter, swings that soar,
Joyful shouts fill the bright air,
Exploring realms like never before,
In this playground, free from care.

Chalk-drawn dreams upon the ground,
Every line a path to take,
Ideas blossom all around,
In the joy that we create.

Tunnels weave through thoughts and play,
Hidden treasures found inside,
In this vibrant, free array,
Imagination is our guide.

Together we can laugh and grow,
In the playground of our mind,
With each idea the chance to glow,
A universe of dreams combined.

Dance of the Muse

Whispers swirl in twilight's embrace,
Each note a brushstroke, a delicate grace.
Footsteps light on soft shadows play,
In the realm where dreams sway.

Spirits twirl in the candle's glow,
Painting wonders, letting thoughts flow.
A tapestry woven in night's soft hue,
Where creation begins anew.

The air fills with magic, electric and bright,
As colors explode in the canvas of night.
Hands reach for the stars, a daring flight,
Connecting the world with pure delight.

In the silence, a story unfolds,
Echoing secrets that never grow old.
The muse dances lightly, igniting a spark,
Guiding the dreamers through shadows dark.

With each spin, a new vision is born,
Inspiration blossoms, like petals of morn.
The dance must continue, forever in flow,
For in moments of magic, the heart learns to grow.

Threads of Enchantment

In the loom of the night, shadows weave,
Stories threaded into the fabric of dreams.
Golden strands glimmer, softly they tease,
Binding the heart with their delicate seams.

Whispers of wonder drift on the breeze,
Each thread a promise, a melody found.
In every knot, a tale is released,
Unity sings in the silence profound.

Colors entwined, a dance so divine,
Orange of sunset, and blue of the sea.
With every pull, creations align,
Magical moments, forever to be.

Embroidered in laughter, stitched with delight,
The tapestry unfolds under midnight's gaze.
Every pattern a memory in soft twilight,
A reflection of life through the misty haze.

So gather the threads, and hold them tight,
For in every woven glimmer, a spark ignites.
Together we craft the enchantment of night,
Bound by the stories, our hearts take flight.

Garden of Ideas

In the garden where thoughts bloom bright,
Seeds of wonder take root in the light.
Colors burst forth with every new dream,
Filling the air with creative esteem.

Butterflies flit on soft whispering winds,
Carrying visions of what might have been.
Petals unfold, each layer a chance,
For the heart to explore, for the soul to dance.

Amidst the green, a symphony plays,
Echoes of laughter and sunlight's rays.
In every corner, new stories unwind,
A treasure of thoughts, beautifully defined.

Beneath the branches, ideas take flight,
Twisting and turning, a marvelous sight.
In the soil of the mind, creativity thrives,
Nurtured by passion, where inspiration derives.

So wander the paths where ideas abound,
Let curiosity's roots dig deep in the ground.
For in this lush garden, our dreams intertwine,
Crafting a future, both vivid and fine.

The Alchemy of Thought

In the cauldron of dreams, ideas collide,
Turning the mundane into pure gold.
Brewing elixirs, where visions abide,
Transformations wrought, both fearless and bold.

With every question, the mind ignites,
Flames of discovery dance in the night.
Metals of theories fused in delight,
Alchemy whispers, revealing insight.

The essence of wonder, bottled in time,
Tasting the future with a hint of the past.
In this sacred space, all thoughts intertwine,
Creating realities, a spell unsurpassed.

As wisdom flows, like rivers of light,
Guiding the seekers through uncharted lands.
In the heart of the storm, clarity's sight,
Crafted with passion, shaped by our hands.

In the laboratory of life, we explore,
Turning base matter into dreams that soar.
The alchemy of thought, a powerful force,
Forever molding our destined course.

Milton Keynes UK
Ingram Content Group UK Ltd.
UKHW020655130824
446895UK00012B/334